Dr. Schulze's 5-Day B Detox Program

✔ **Eliminate constipation and promote regular, healthy and complete bowel movements**

✔ **A powerful intestinal vacuum that draws out old toxic fecal matter**

✔ **Have more energy, feel lighter and have a flatter stomach**

A sluggish, swollen bowel can compress a nearby area, causing disease, or emit infection and toxins, which can affect any area of the body. This explains why about 80% of Dr. Schulze's patients healed their problems by cleaning out their colons before he ever did any specialized treatment for their problem. No matter how far removed the problem seems from the colon, cleanse the bowel first and see what happens. If you're like Dr. Schulze's patients, you will be thrilled with the results.

Dr. Schulze's
OFFICIAL PUBLICATIONS
Since 1979

Published by Natural Healing Publications
P.O. Box 9459, Marina del Rey, California 90295
1-877-TEACH-ME (832-2463)

Library of Congress Catalog Card Number: PENDING
25 WAYS TO HAVE THE CLEANEST BOWEL

ISBN: 0-9671567-1-8

WARNING

This book is published under the First Amendment of the United States Constitution, which grants the right to discuss openly and freely all matters of public concern and to express viewpoints no matter how controversial or unaccepted they may be. However, Medical groups and Pharmaceutical companies have finally infiltrated and violated our sacred constitution. Therefore we are forced to give you the following WARNINGS:

If you are ill or have been diagnosed with any disease, please consult a medical doctor before attempting any natural healing program.

Many foods, herbs or other natural substances can occasionally have dangerous allergic reactions or side effects in some people. People have even died from allergic reactions to peanuts and strawberries.

Any one of the programs in this book could be potentially dangerous, even lethal. Especially if you are seriously ill.

Therefore, any natural method you learn about in this book may cause harm, instead of the benefit you seek. ASK YOUR DOCTOR FIRST, but remember that the vast majority of doctors have no education in natural healing methods and herbal medicine. They will probably discourage you from trying any of the programs.

"The first and most important step for preventing and healing disease is bowel cleansing."

–Dr. Richard Schulze

TABLE OF CONTENTS

TABLE OF CONTENTS

INTRODUCTION

"Never, never, never underestimate the healing power of colon cleansing." –Dr. Richard Schulze

I remember when my older brother got his first car. It was a 1950 Ford station wagon. Of course it didn't run. What kid's first car did? So it sat in our driveway and we would sit in it dreaming of the day when we would be burning rubber down the highway. Being more mechanically inclined, I did most of the work on it to get it running.

I used to be able to open up the hood, sit on a front fender with my feet and legs actually dangling inside the engine compartment and work on the engine, change spark plugs, whatever. Get the picture? Big car, big hood, little engine, lots of room. Nowadays, I open up the hood of my 2001 Ford Expedition and I just shut it right back up. Every square inch under the hood is jammed, packed with engine parts, power pumps, wires, hoses, pipes, and filters. It is too complex, and even if I understood it, there is NO ROOM to work on it. NO SPACE!

What's my point? I used to think our anatomy was like my brother's 1950 Ford. You know, a lung up here, a kidney way down there, a bowel in the middle, with lots of room. Then one day in school I examined my first cadaver and WOW, what an enlightening experience.  The human anatomy is not like my brother's 1950 Ford at all; it is like my 2001 Ford. Every square inch is packed with something and everything is touching something else. This body of ours must have had some incredible engineer. Everything has its place and THERE IS NO EXTRA ROOM! If one organ swells or gets bigger, then another organ (usually the one next to the swollen one) gets squeezed, compressed or crushed. Organs don't work so well when they are crushed and the blood, lymphatic, nerve and general circulation gets interrupted. Every organ needs good circulation to get nutrition in and get waste out in order to be healthy. Squeezed and compressed organs get sick.

Now, the entire colon is so big that it is connected to, touches, sits next to or is in the vicinity of every major organ in the human body except the brain. It also touches most of your major blood vessels and nerves. Constipation causes the colon to literally swell, expand and even herniate. Remember that the leading medical books told us that all of us store too much fecal matter and have this happening inside of us. So when an area of the colon gets constipated and swells, it compresses and crushes the organ next to it. This could be the lungs, the heart, the liver and gall bladder, the pancreas, the kidneys and adrenals, the uterus, the prostate – again, almost every major organ in the body. This is simply why a constipated, swollen colon can cause an almost endless amount of seemingly unrelated diseases and problems, and I haven't even discussed toxic build-up in the colon that literally infects and poisons nearby organs.

The majority of patients in my clinic were female. Many women could never understand the relationship between their painful periods, PMS, menstrual irregularity, vaginal infections, infertility, menopausal problems, problems during pregnancy, whatever, and their constipation until I explained that their sigmoid colon wraps around the uterus and that their ovaries are literally attached to the colon. The cure for almost every female problem in my clinic besides my Female Formulae was a good bowel cleansing.

Men, don't try to wriggle out of this one. It's the same for you and your prostate, which is attached to the part of your colon that swells and gets constipated most often, crushing and infecting the prostate.

The point is there is NO EXTRA SPACE in your body. If your bowel swells due to constipation and bowel pockets, another organ gets pinched, if not crushed.

What's the bottom line? A sluggish, constipated, swollen bowel, retaining pounds of old fecal matter, can either compress a nearby area, causing disease, or emit infection and toxins which can affect and infect any area of the body. This explains why many of my patients healed so many of their unrelated problems by cleaning out their colons before I ever did any specialized treatment for their problem.

Dr. Richard Schulze

1 WHY SHOULD I DO DR. SCHULZE'S 5-DAY BOWEL DETOX PROGRAM?

I have literally traveled around the world in search of what a normal bowel movement and bowel habit should be like. Now, how many people can say that? I have traveled from the remote jungles of Central America to India, China, almost everywhere, to discover what is normal because I knew I wasn't going to find normal in New York, California and not even in Iowa. I wanted to see primitive people living in rural, non-industrialized areas, living simple rural lives under very little stress, getting moderate amounts of exercise and eating simple natural diets of locally foraged food. These relaxed primitive people all seem to have one bowel movement within 20 to 30 minutes after each major meal that they ate. They just squat, it rapidly comes out within a minute, and they are done. No library of magazines, no squeezing, straining, grunting, meditation or prayer. It just comes out effortlessly. They seem to average between 2 and 4 bowel movements a day or 14 to 28 bowel movements a week compared to the average American's bowel habit of 1 bowel movement every 3 to 5 days or 2 to 3 bowel movements a week. **I figured this puts the Average American about 70,000 bowel movements short in their lifetime!** The consistency of your bowel movements should be soft and unformed like peanut butter or soft serve frozen ice cream. Occasionally they can be a bit chunky depending on what you ate and how well you chewed it, but in any case they should NOT be formed and they should be light in color. I remember as a kid my dad only went once a week on Sundays. He would take the entire Sunday paper in the bathroom and be in there for hours. When he came out the room smelled like someone died. I would then take my place at the throne after him and squeeze hard for my once-a-week bowel movement. Eventually I would blast out some small black balls as hard as granite. My dad would come into the bathroom to wipe me, but my fecal matter was so dry and hard there was nothing on the toilet paper. I remember my dad remarking, "Now that's a good poop, no wiping, like it's wrapped in cellophane," and I would leave for a week thinking I did a good job. If you need a library in your bathroom, you know, like a stack of magazines on the hamper, then you are constipated. If you drink coffee, well, if you stop, you will also probably stop having bowel movements too.

2 WHAT IS THE FOOD PROGRAM WHILE DOING YOUR 5-DAY BOWEL DETOX PROGRAM?

The reason for doing my 5-Day BOWEL Detox Program in the first place is to first get your bowel to work better, more frequently, and more completely, to empty the waste out of your body. And secondly, it is to clean out old waste that has accumulated in your bowel. The reason your bowel isn't working well and has accumulated waste is because of what you ate. Food that is difficult to digest and assimilate and food that is difficult to eliminate. Processed foods, cooked foods, junk foods. So it only makes sense that when you're doing a bowel cleansing program, you wouldn't want to be consuming those foods that caused your bowel problem in the first place. So although you can eat a varied food program while you're doing the bowel cleanse, it would be nice to not be consuming the food that caused the bowel problem in the first place. Some people think they have to fast, or just drink juices. That's not true. Other people would like to do the cleanse and not really modify their food program much. That's possible. So I would say for the average person you can go ahead and consume food. But just make it so that during the two weeks that you're doing the 5-Day BOWEL Detox Program that you're consuming clean food, the type of food that's loaded with fiber. Preferably a vegetarian diet. Fruits, vegetables, nuts, legumes, seeds, and grains and sprouts. This type of food is loaded with fiber, loaded with nutrition, and it's not going to add to your bowel problem. In fact, it's going to aid the BOWEL Detox Program in scrubbing out your intestines. What you want to stay away from are refined flour products, like bread and pasta. Those things you could glue wallpaper to the wall with. And you want to stay away from animal products. Why? Because all animal products— beef, chicken, pork, fish, eggs, dairy. . . everything that had a face on it, or came from anything with a face on it, has zero fiber. All this is going to do is slow down your bowel. All animal (fiber-less) food is going to do is cause further constipation and further plaquing in your bowel. So the main food program you would want to follow would be a clean vegetarian food program. Now, if you want to assist the bowel cleanse or if you have had chronic problems with constipation or chronic problems with accumulated waste in your bowel, go ahead and assist it by making the food program even lighter. Have a few days of juice flushing in there. Go ahead and consume food for a few days on your normal vegetarian, healthy, clean food program. Then have a few days of raw foods. Then have a few days of juice cleansing. Then go back to raw foods, then go back to the vegetarian diet. That would assist your cleanse, and certainly you can juice cleanse for the whole two weeks that you're doing this bowel program. But for the majority of people, just a clean, healthy, fiber-full vegetarian food program is the best way to eat while you're doing my 5-Day BOWEL Detox Program.

3 WHAT IF I AM AFRAID OF DOING THE PROGRAM?

For all of you out there who are afraid to start my 5-Day BOWEL Detox Program, afraid you might not make it to the bathroom, don't be afraid. Your fear should be about going to a doctor. Your fear should be about ever having to go to a hospital. Believe me, the American Medical Association and the pharmaceutical industry have done a great job in brainwashing you if you're afraid to begin your own self-treatment, create a healthier lifestyle and use some herbs to heal yourself. That's exactly where they want you. My job is to empower you. Come on, we're talking herbology and Natural Healing here. We're not talking about nuclear physics or advanced calculus. This is simple, and it's your God-given right to heal and cleanse and detoxify and build your strength and help yourself and your family members. So break free of that iron-clenching fist of the AMA and the drug companies that want you to be stupid and led like sheep to the slaughter in the hospital. Believe me, that's what they want. I had thousands of patients in my practice, and believe me, I cleansed all their bowels, and they weren't a bunch of out-of-work bohemians. They all worked for a living. In fact, almost all of them were in the television and movie and music industry, and they couldn't just say, hey everybody, stop everything, I gotta go to the bathroom for about three hours. They worked regular jobs, they were regular people, and believe me, they all cleaned their bowels and they didn't have to take time off of work. Granted, when you're cleansing your bowels you will notice that you have to go a lot more often. But it's not a big deal. It'll be very quick and complete. In fact, even if you go to the bathroom one extra time a day, I guarantee you, you'll be spending a lot less time in that bathroom. You can throw out all the magazines, because you won't have time to read anything. You'll sit down, you'll have your bowel movement, and you'll be out of there in two minutes flat. So don't use time as an excuse not to do the program.

4 WHAT IF I EXPERIENCE CRAMPING WHILE ON THE CLEANSE?

For those of you experiencing stomach cramps from taking the **Intestinal Formula #1**, relax. Any time you use a muscle that hasn't worked in a long time, you're going to feel it. This is no different than if you go to the gym for a week's worth of new workout sessions after years of a sedate lifestyle and no exercise. Believe me, you're going to feel it. The analogy I always used with my patients 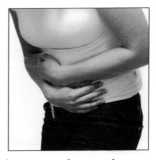 in the clinic is, imagine you have an old car in the garage that maybe you inherited from your dad and you haven't started it up in a few years, and you decide one day to go out, charge the battery, and crank it up. Is it going to run smooth at first? Of course not. It's going to shake, it's going to rattle, it's going to backfire from the carburetor and it's going to smoke from the exhaust. And then maybe in ten or fifteen minutes it's going to smooth out and run nice. So remember, when you first start taking the **Intestinal Formula #1**, you might have some cramping in your lower abdomen. You might feel it when you sit on the toilet the next day and that bowel starts to really work, the muscles contract, and you have a great bowel movement. That's great. You're alive. Remember, like that car, you might shake and sputter and skip and backfire and smoke and even stink a few minutes when you first start the bowel up, but I guarantee you, in a few weeks, in a month, that bowel is going to work and you're going to be absolutely thrilled you started working on healing and strengthening it.

5 I'VE TRIED OTHER COLON CLEANSES AND THEY DIDN'T WORK. HOW DO I KNOW YOURS IS GOING TO WORK?

In my clinic I found that generally as patients came into me and I'd say, we're going to do some herbal therapy, they'd say, I've tried herbs and they don't work. And I used to get irritated by that. And then I went out and tried the majority of herbs, and I thought, they really don't work. And it's not that the herbs don't work. I'm not blaming the herbal manufacturers, because they've just been beat up by the government for the last fifty years in America, but the idea became, don't make something that can cause any negative effects in anybody. Well, what that means is creating a product that won't cause any effect at all. So in the clinic I dealt with people differently. I figured we needed something strong. For some of my patients I had to actually get out the old Seventeenth and Eighteenth Century veterinarian books and come up with laxatives that were used for two thousand pound animals, like horses. That's the degree of constipation that we have in America today. I had patients that went once a month, and that wasn't unheard of. I had patients that went once every other month, a thirty-eight year old woman that went six times a year. And then I had a record-breaker, a young lady from Northern California, who went only three times during her pregnancy, and then two times outside that, so we're talking five times a year. And my ultimate record-breaker was two bowel movements a year. So basically I concocted an emergency, full-strength formula that my brother originally named depth charges, because I gave it to him years ago and he said his bowel is still working great to this day. So don't worry about what any other herbal cleanses did or didn't do for you. Just trust me and try my 5-Day Bowel Detox Program.

6 HOW MANY TIMES SHOULD I DO YOUR 5-DAY BOWEL DETOX PROGRAM?

A lot of people wonder how many times they should do my 5-Day BOWEL Detox Program. The answer is easy, and it applies to all cleansing. My patients, once they were well, once they were feeling great, with energy and vitality, and free of disease, I would suggest that they do a cleansing routine once every season. So that's four times a year for a week. And that cleansing routine does include both the **Intestinal Formula #1** and the **Intestinal Formula #2.**

7 SHOULD I DO THE 5-DAY BOWEL DETOX PROGRAM WHEN DOING EITHER THE LIVER OR KIDNEY 5-DAY DETOX PROGRAMS?

A lot of people ask if they should be taking the **Intestinal Formula #1** and **#2** during the Liver and Kidney Flushes, and the answer is yes. Any time you're fasting, any time you're flushing, when you're doing your seasonal cleanse, any time you're cleaning yourself out, the foundation of any cleansing is the bowel program. You need to keep that bowel working and activated so that any debris that you're cleaning out of your body can get out immediately. Whatever program you're doing, make sure you're cleansing your bowel. I saw many patients who had gone through many types of detoxification programs, and in the middle of those programs got themselves into deep trouble and came running to my clinic for help. And I was amazed at how many different so-called hip or sophisticated cleansing programs did not include getting the bowel working. I know some groups that put you in saunas and have you drink liquids, and that's great, that can really purge poisons out of your body, but if you haven't had a bowel movement in a week, you're going to be in a lot of trouble. The foundation of any cleansing program or routine has to be getting that bowel working. In fact, it should have been working long before you even thought about another detoxification. Remember, in my clinic I said you had to earn a cleanse by doing your homework up front.

8 CAN I STILL DO THE 5-DAY BOWEL DETOX PROGRAM IF I'M PREGNANT OR NURSING, AND IF I'M NURSING IS IT HARMFUL TO THE BABY?

No, it is not harmful to the baby, and yes, you can do it while you're pregnant. In fact, you can do any of my programs. In extreme situations, where Mom was going to die before delivering the child (in other words, maybe Mom was given a month or two to live and the baby wasn't ready for five months) I even had moms do the Incurables Program, my thirty day intensive cleansing and detox program, because Mom was going to die and we were going to lose the baby. But in a normal situation, yes, Mom can do any of these programs while she's pregnant. You just  want to use your common sense. Certainly **SuperFood Plus** is the best for pregnancy and for nursing, because you're feeding either the fetus or that baby the best blood and then, once it's born, the best milk that you can imagine. Because you're fortifying your blood and your milk with **SuperFood Plus**.

The **Intestinal Formula #1**, well, here's where the common sense comes in. You shouldn't be sending yourself into an extensive, intensive, cathartic bowel movement in your eighth and a half month of pregnancy, unless you want to bring on labor. That said, you can use your **Intestinal Formula #1** even in your third trimester, that's no problem. Just don't cause some major bowel catharsis. Keep it simple and lower your dosage.

Once you have your baby, if you want to use your **Intestinal Formula #1**, that's fine. But remember, any herb you take will get through your milk into your baby on a reduced level. So you're also going to be treating your baby, too, which is great, because if your baby has an infection, you can take high dosages of **Echinacea Plus,** and it will get through the breast milk into your child. So yes, you can do all the programs when you're pregnant and when you're nursing. Just use your head and your good common sense.

9 WHAT IS THE DOSAGE FOR INTESTINAL FORMULA #1?

Taking the **Intestinal Formula #1** is simple. Unless you want to learn the laws of jet propulsion, start with one capsule. It's a strong formula. The best way to take it is during or just after dinner. When you have some food in your stomach, take just one capsule. The next morning when you wake up, you might notice a dramatic difference in your bowel movements. If not, if you don't look at that toilet in amazement at what came out of you, then this evening with dinner take two capsules, and wait and see what happens the next day. You keep increasing by one capsule every day, and you'll know when you achieve the right dosage. You'll feel it. You'll feel that colon, that large muscle in your lower abdomen, beginning to work and removing all the bowel material.

10 I'VE ALREADY WORKED UP TO A HIGH NUMBER OF THE INTESTINAL FORMULA #1 AND I'M AFRAID TO TAKE MORE. WHAT DO I DO?

A lot of people with sluggish bowels work up to a high number of pills and are afraid to take any more. Don't be afraid. What we need to fear is all the health problems and diseases and illnesses that are caused by constipation. There's no limit to the amount of **Intestinal Formula #1** you can take. I received a letter from one man in Hawaii who had to take forty-five capsules before his bowel opened up. And after twenty-four hours of sitting on the toilet this man lost fifty-two pounds. That's right. Fifty-two pounds of fecal matter! Now, this was a heavy man, well over four hundred pounds. His wife was the one who told me this story, and she said to me, you know, Dr. Schulze, I always knew he was full of crap. And she was right. As far as I know, forty-eight capsules is the record, and I doubt if it will take you that much. But don't be afraid to take as many capsules as you need to get your bowels working.

11 I'M HAVING TWO TO THREE BOWEL MOVEMENTS A DAY, BUT NOT THIRTY MINUTES AFTER EACH MEAL LIKE YOU SUGGEST. IS THIS OK?

Hey, remember, I'm going for perfection here. Like I said, when I examined primitive people who lived very natural lives, they would eat, and after every major meal, within about thirty minutes, their bowel would move. That's what I'd like to see, and that's the way most of my healthy patients' bowels work most of the time. Not every time. Not everybody within thirty minutes evacuates their bowel. But that is a goal that you are going for. That is definitely a good goal, that at least one of your major meals that you eat during the day, whether in the morning, evening or midday, that thirty minutes afterward you have a bowel movement. That's when you know your bowel is getting really healthy and strong.

12 IF I'M HAVING A BOWEL MOVEMENT THIRTY MINUTES AFTER A MEAL, ISN'T THAT TOO FAST FOR ALL THIS FOOD TO BE MOVING IN AND OUT OF ME?

Well, not really, because the bowel movement that you're having thirty minutes after a meal is not the material from the meal that you just ate. Say you have a bowel movement thirty minutes after having your dinner. At best, that's your lunch. Probably, most likely, it's your breakfast. Maybe even the dinner from the night before. But it's not the food that you just ate coming out of you. The reason is that when you start chewing food, you excrete saliva, and you start out a peristalsis action, a muscular wave in your esophagus that works its way down to your stomach that also squeezes to help digest the food that you're eating.

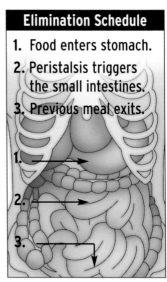

Elimination Schedule

1. Food enters stomach.
2. Peristalsis triggers the small intestines.
3. Previous meal exits.

But at the same time a peristalsis is triggered in your small intestine. There's a triggering reaction, and that starts helping you digest, assimilate, and eliminate the meal that you ate before. And that usually starts a wave going of peristalsis or muscular movement, contraction, and action in your colon which will start you to eliminate the previous meal or two meals after you eat your current meal. So what am I saying? When you have a meal and a bowel movement thirty minutes later, you are not excreting the food that you just ate. It's from one or two, if not three, meals ago.

13 I'M EXPERIENCING A LOT MORE GAS WHEN I USE YOUR INTESTINAL FORMULA #1. IS THAT OK, OR AM I ALLERGIC?

Well, no, you're not allergic, and that's perfectly OK. Remember, I always use the analogy, if you had an old car in your garage and you hadn't started it in years and you went out and started cranking the engine you might get explosions out of the carburetor or backfires out of the rear end, and it would shake and sputter, but after about fifteen minutes it's going to hum, it's going to run well. Well, this is just like your bowel. When you have more gas it means that the **Intestinal Formula #1** is breaking up old deposits of fecal matter, stuff that's in there for years, the fudgsicle you ate when you were fourteen, all those candy bars you had on Halloween when you were five. Let me tell you, there's a lot of old material in everybody's bowel, and the **Intestinal Formula #1** breaks up that old fecal matter, that old toxic poisonous material. And when it does that you can often get a little more gas. If you want to help relieve the gas, use my **Digestive Tonic** along with the **Intestinal Formula #1**, and that will give you more gas-relieving capability. Take a couple droppersful in about an ounce of water, knock it back, and that will help move the gas on.

14 CAN I TAKE INTESTINAL FORMULA #1 INDEFINITELY?

Most people start taking the **Intestinal Formula #1** and feel great. They love it. They're having regular, frequent, complete, full bowel movements, probably for the first time in their life. They feel great, they've lost weight, their tummy's flat, but then they wonder, can I take this formula for a while or a month or six months or a year, or even indefinitely? And of course the answer is very simple. To poop or not to poop... that is the question. The downsides of constipation are endless, are infinite. You can have sickness, illness, disease, immune weakness, low energy, back problems, headaches, leg pain, menstrual irregularity, hormone imbalance, emotional problems, bad digestion, poor assimilation... numerous diseases, including diverticulosis and herniation of the intestine due to impaction. Modern medicine says that a hundred percent of Americans, before they die, are going to have herniated intestines due to constipation. I saw hundreds of patients that developed cancer in the bowel simply because of constipation. I also saw every disease, every illness, no matter what it was, helped by cleaning out the bowel. You may think that your disease or your problem is totally unrelated to your bowel, but let me tell you, the old natural healers knew it, and they were right. You clean out your bowel and miracles can happen. Now, for those whose diet and lifestyle inhibit them from having regular bowel movements, or those who have inherited sleepy and sluggish bowels, I couldn't suggest using this formula enough to get your regular bowel movements until the time comes when your bowel works perfectly on its own. What's the downside? I don't know of any. Besides the cost of the herbs, there's none that I'm aware of. Rumors suggest that constant use of cathartic herbs will become addicting, but I've never, ever seen this. Constant use of cathartic herbs with no lifestyle change, well, if you want to continue to poop, you better keep taking the herbs. But on the other hand, I've seen thousands of people worldwide, including myself, that used **Intestinal Formula #1** for years and then, when their lifestyle was corrected and adjusted enough, the bowel started working naturally two to three times a day on its own. I'm one of those. I took the formula for over ten years before my lifestyle, my exercise program, my new emotional program and all of the good things I was doing kicked in enough for me to feel better and have those regular two to three bowel movements a day where my bowel moved thirty minutes after each major meal. So it can take some time, especially if you have years of hard living or bad living habits or, again, have inherited a very weak, sleepy bowel. Once my patients would start having regular bowel movements without the formula, the only time they used **Intestinal Formula #1** again was during episodes of constipation, usually Thanksgiving, Christmas, and any time the family gets together and eats, or when they traveled... any time they threw off their system and it resulted in constipation. Then you can use **Intestinal Formula #1** on a temporary basis, but believe me, my patients didn't get addicted. I always say it's like going to the gym. If you do isolated biceps curls, that makes your biceps stronger, and when they're stronger they work better. So, so much for this rumor of addiction.

15 WHY CAN'T I CONTINUE HAVING REGULAR BOWEL MOVEMENTS WHEN I STOP TAKING THE INTESTINAL FORMULA #1?

Well, there's a couple reasons for this. One is your bowel is not healed and strong enough yet. Remember, taking **Intestinal Formula #1** is like sending your colon to the gym and doing an isolated biceps curl. Every time you take that formula it works the muscles of your bowel, creating more peristalsis. So every time you take that formula, your bowel gets cleaner and stronger. But it doesn't happen overnight. Some people need to take the formula for months, others for up to a year. Personally,

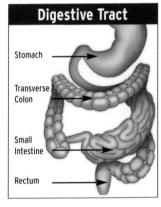

I had to take that formula for twelve years before my bowel (because I inherited a very bad bowel) worked perfectly on its own. And now I only take the formula maybe once or twice a year, maybe if I'm traveling (because that can cause constipation), or if I go to too many parties in a row, have some food that really isn't on my day-to-day program and want to get it out of my body. But that's the main reason. Also, another reason is maybe your lifestyle, especially your food program, hasn't changed enough yet, or you haven't had those changes made for a long enough period. Because, remember, so many things also affect your peristalsis, like the type of food you're eating. Is it live enough? Is it raw enough? Does it have enough fiber? Does it have enough enzymes? The more you get towards that good, organic fruit, vegetable, vegan food program, the better your bowel is going to work. Also, lifestyle changes. If you're happy, your bowel is going to work much better than if you're unhappy. Maybe you sit in an office all day long, and that certainly isn't going to promote the bowel to move as much as it would if you were working outside and up and moving. So, again, the two reasons that when you stop the 5-Day BOWEL Detox Program that your bowel stops working is, one, your bowel isn't strong enough yet, so continue the program, and two, your food program and your lifestyle changes need to be more dramatic or need to be better for a longer period of time. So don't stop them, either. In fact, make your food program cleaner, get in more exercise, and make your lifestyle changes, keep up with your **Intestinal Formula #1**, and you, like all my patients, will end up having a perfect bowel.

16 CAN I START TAKING THE INTESTINAL FORMULA #2 RIGHT AWAY?

Do not start taking the **Intestinal Formula #2** until you get your bowels working. I suggest, in all the literature, that you use the **Intestinal Formula #1** for a week and then, as your bowels are regulated, you start with the #2. But do not start the **Intestinal Formula #2** until your bowels are regulated. So for those of you who are constipated or who have had years of constipation or maybe have inherently weak bowels, don't be in any hurry. Nobody should be in any hurry to start **Intestinal Formula #2.** Stay on **Intestinal Formula #1** until you are having regular, frequent bowel movements that put a smile on your face every morning, and you're starting to have bowel movements even at other times during the day after your meals. And when you're feeling really good about your bowel and the way it's working, then you start the **Intestinal Formula #2.**

17 WHY DOES INTESTINAL FORMULA #2 CONSTIPATE ME?

Some people take the **Intestinal Formula #2** and find that it constipates them, and there's a few reasons for this. First off, remember, the whole time you're using the **Intestinal Formula #2** you should also be using the **Intestinal Formula #1.** In fact, if you read the directions you should be using more of it than you normally need, because **Intestinal Formula #2** is the great drawing, cleansing, detoxifying formula for the bowel. It's going to go in there and pull out everything. But on its own, inherently, **Intestinal Formula #2** is constipating for most people, especially if you suffer from some form of constipation. So if you just take **Intestinal Formula #2** on its own, it may just solidify your bowels and stop them from working. The first step is getting a good dosage of **Intestinal Formula #1** down, to where your bowels are working and you're very happy with the frequency and completeness of your bowel movements, and then increase it by a capsule or maybe even two, and then begin the week-long process of **Intestinal Formula #2.**

18 DO I HAVE TO CONSUME THE WHOLE BOTTLE OF INTESTINAL FORMULA #2?

Yes. **Intestinal Formula #2** is designed for one person to consume in one week, and it's not until you finish the bottle that you finish the cleanse. If you are using **Intestinal Formula #2** capsules, your goal is to take 10 capsules 5 times per day for the next 5 days. That is 50 capsules a day. If you are using **Intestinal Formula #2** packets, then simply take 5 packets 5 times a day for the next 5 days. Remember, during this program on average you will be taking **Intestinal Formula #2** (capsules or packets) every 2 to 3 hours throughout the day.

19 I'M TAKING YOUR INTESTINAL FORMULA #2, BUT ISN'T THIS BLACK DRINK A BIT RADICAL?

Well, let me tell you something. It doesn't taste black, and it doesn't taste radical. Some people are so brainwashed by modern medicine that they begin to think that herbal medicine and Natural Healing is radical. They think that medical doctors and the practice of modern medicine is normal, is rational, but that herbs and Natural Healing is radical. People who think this are the living proof of the success of one of the greatest con jobs in American history. And this con job is to sell medicine to a society of people, but scare them out of ever taking their healing into their own hands. Let me tell you something, Kidney dialysis, that's radical. That should be in a vampire movie. Liver and heart transplants, that's radical. The fact that even medical universities like Stanford say that the human body should live a hundred and twenty-five years but we're all dying in our early seventies... that's radical. Let me tell you radical. I had a patient who was in her early thirties, and she had an aggressively growing brain tumor. The doctors did a surgery, and they opened up her skull and they scooped most of the tumor out but they couldn't get it all. They closed her back up where she lied in intensive care for almost thirty days. She said she was in the worst pain of her entire life. She was totally paralyzed, couldn't talk, couldn't communicate, couldn't even blink her eyes, and she said it felt like someone had hot nails driving through her head, and every moment of every day, every second, she was screaming silently to herself. That's radical. Let me tell you, I had a patient who had a tumor in her rectum, and the doctor said hey, let us do some pinpoint, laser-guided smart bomb radiation treatment and we'll get rid of that tumor. I tried to explain to her that radiation treatment is not that smart and not that well-guided and that she could end up with a horrible burn and that we should try Natural Healing, but no, she went ahead and had her radiation treatment on that tumor, and two days later when she was having a bowel movement, the bowel material came out her vagina because they burned out the wall between her rectum and her vagina. Friends, that's radical. Get with it here. There is nothing radical about going out into your backyard and finding a few plants that God has provided for our food and for our medicine. This is not radical. Natural Healing and water treatments and exercise and being happy and having a great spiritual life, this is not radical. Mutilating surgery, burning toxic radiation, killer chemicals called chemotherapy, this is radical. **Intestinal Formula #2** has a little charcoal, a little fruit pectin, and a few herbs. This formula may be black in color, but mix it with juice, it will taste just fine, it will clear years of poisons out of your bowel, and I assure you, it is nowhere near a radical treatment.

20 IF I HAVE CROHN'S OR COLITIS OR IRRITABLE BOWEL SYNDROME, HOW DO I APPROACH THE CLEANSE?

For those of you with Crohn's disease or colitis or irritable bowel syndrome, do not start with the **Intestinal Formula #1.** **Intestinal Formula #1** is for about ninety-eight percent of the people out there, the people with sluggish bowels, maybe a history of constipation, but who do not have a bowel movement

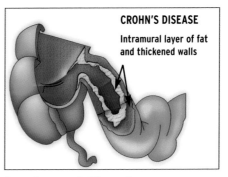

CROHN'S DISEASE

Intramural layer of fat and thickened walls

twenty to thirty minutes after each major meal. The other two percent, those who are having too many bowel movements, don't need to increase their bowel movements, and that's what the **Intestinal Formula #1** does. So instead of using the **Intestinal Formula #1,** just go right to the **Intestinal Formula #2.** If you're one of those two percent, you'll love it. You'll think it puts the fire out in your bowel. It'll soothe the irritated tissue, reduce the inflammation in your colon, and solidify the diarrhea-like bowel movements. You'll feel wonderful. Believe me, it will be a blessing in your life to start on the **Intestinal Formula #2.**

21 IS IT CONSTIPATION THAT CAUSES A FECAL ENCASEMENT?

Yes. Basically, as Americans, we're not big on fiber. We love meat, dairy, chicken, fish, eggs, cheese, and the first thing people have to realize is, animal equals zero fiber. Anything that came from an animal has no fiber, which means it sits in your bowel, and it really won't go anywhere until you consume something that has fiber, which pushes it out. So the good old American food program of bacon and eggs is literally stuck down there. I had patients that during a bowel cleanse, after having already done three or four previous cleanses, would eliminate the entire casing of the inside of their bowel. I'm talking five feet long here, and they'd eliminate it in one bowel movement. And they'd be frightened, because they thought they were losing their colon, not just eliminating the old toxic liner. And you could even see the sacks on it; they would come out at the same time. But during normal bowel cleansing, those diverticuli don't get emptied. It takes a little bit of advanced bowel cleansing to get rid of them.

22 DO I NEED TO BE TAKING ACIDOPHILUS?

For those of you worried about taking acidophilus or lacto-bacillus bacteria after doing the bowel cleanse, I ask you this: Who said that my program took the flora out of your bowel? If you're on a good food program with some nice raw fruits and vegetables and sprouts and soaked beans and all those good things, you shouldn't have any problem with your intestinal flora. And if you think you do, think about fermented veggies and garlic.

Garlic is wonderful for your intestinal flora, and raw sauerkrauts and Anne Wigmore's Rejuvelac, and fermented soy yogurts and seed cheeses, and all those wonderful things that you can use to get bacteria back in your bowel. And if you're really worried or have a history of problems, then sure, you  can take some bacteria, like various lacto-bacillus strains, but when you do, please stay away from the ones that are made with dairy products. Use the ones—I see them all the time—that are made with apple juice and other great foods instead of getting near all that cow juice that's just going to constipate you and cause problems all over again. And now that you've cleaned out your bowel, you don't want that. But if you need to, or if you feel you need to, sure, you can take some added bacteria to help your intestinal flora.

23 ARE THERE THINGS YOU EAT THAT ACTUALLY STAY IN YOUR COLON FOR YEARS AND YEARS?

Yes. It's actually a medical fact more than a Natural Healing fact. The Merck Manual is the American standard, if not the international standard, of diagnoses of disease. It's produced by Merck Research Laboratories, one of the largest drug companies in America, and it's a standard medical text of disease used around the world. Every doctor has one. And their statistics say that in 1950 ten percent of all Americans had diverticulosis, or herniated sacs, in their colon caused by the pressure and stuffing of constipation, where fecal matter literally pushes into a weak part, or a balloon, in the wall of the muscle of the bowel and stays there. But in 1955 they raised that to 15%. And in 1972 they went up to 30%, and in the 1987 edition they said just about half of Americans have diverticulosis or herniated sacs in their colon. And in the most recent edition of the Merck Manual, it says if people live long enough, every American will have herniated bowel pockets or diverticuli (which are just like a weak spot on a balloon or a rubber tire where it bulges), and they get filled with fecal matter. And basic common sense will tell you it just stays in there. In fact, the whole colon can get encased in fecal matter in advanced constipation, to where it looks like a rusty pipe, an old steel or galvanized pipe in your house, and when you look through it you can only see a small hole.

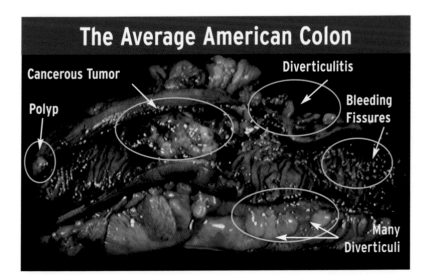

The Average American Colon

Cancerous Tumor

Diverticulitis

Polyp

Bleeding Fissures

Many Diverticuli

24 HOW CAN AN HERB STIMULATE A SLUGGISH BOWEL THAT'S BEEN A CHRONIC PROBLEM?

It's great. I'm always amazed by how many people say, I don't get it, how do herbs work? And I think, I don't get it, how do they not? We don't question food, do we? All food and herbs and plants and trees and barks and berries and resins and strawberries and blueberries and anything that grows on this planet contain chemicals. Some of these chemicals are nutritional, like vitamins and minerals and enzymes. Other chemicals are stronger, like essential oils and alkaloids, and they're very medicinal. All the original classic prescription drugs in America were isolated from chemicals found in plants. Over fifty percent of the drugs used today were originally chemicals found in herbs. Herbs simply work off chemicals. There's a group of chemicals called anthroquinones, and there's a particular anthroquinone, called Emodin, which is in certain herbs like the aloes that grow equatorially around the world, or Senna pods and leaves, which are famous throughout recorded history as laxatives in the Nile Delta. And then there's Cascara Sagrada, which is our California plant. These all contain the anthroquinone Emodin, and Emodin, when it gets inside your bowel and touches your colon wall, actually makes the muscle move. It stimulates that muscle to move. It's kind of like going to the gym. You're strengthening that muscle by stimulating it to move. And it stimulates it to move so much that in one naturopathic school we took a bowel out of a dead person and when we smeared the different Emodin herbs in it, the bowel actually contracted. So hence comes my statement that I've been accused of making a few times, that I can even get a dead person to have a bowel movement. And it comes from the fact that I don't need any participation from the patient. These herbs are powerful enough to make the bowel contract and work. It starts that muscular peristalsis specifically in the colon. So it's going to make your bowel work tomorrow, and I don't care what you're eating, drinking, or thinking. We'll get right, but that might take a month or two. Right now, tomorrow, I need your bowel to work. So I made the **Intestinal Formula #1** in the clinic to guarantee me that I could get my patients' bowels to work regardless of whether or not they had corrected anything yet. I had to get the elimination channels, the channels of waste removal, working in the body, and the herbs are what did it.

25 BESIDES HERBS, WHAT ELSE CAN I DO TO STIMULATE MY BOWEL?

People always forget the simple things that our grandparents knew. Often with patients I would just get them to soak some prunes. I mean, when my plum trees ripen here in my orchard I don't get one a day, I get four thousand in an hour. And then the tree is bare three days later. So often what fruit is telling you is gorge on it, have massive amounts for a short period of time, do a plum cleanse. With prunes, you can just soak them in water, put them in a blender, add some apple juice, and for some people that's enough.

I found that for my patients most of them needed something to jump-start the engine, something to get that bowel working effectively. But there's basically six natural ways to get your colon working. The first one is to drink more liquid. The bowel can't work properly without a minimum of two quarts, or sixty-four ounces of liquid, in a day. The fastest way to get your bowel to stop working is to dehydrate. Your bowel needs water in order to process the fecal matter and get it out of your body. The second one is to eat more fiber. Fiber makes your bowel work. Sludge doesn't. Animal foods are sludge. Refined flour products are sludge. We have to eat more fruits, vegetables, grains, and sprouts. Adding more fiber and drinking more liquid can make your bowel work tremendously better. And the least altered something is from its natural form (the more raw it is), the more powerful it is. Then there are the natural laxative foods, like fruit. Fruits are great. Apples, dates, figs, bananas, just about any food that contains liquid. Stay away from the dehydrated fruits if you're constipated, because they suck moisture out of your body and we're trying to add more in. The fourth way is to move your body. Just walking creates peristalsis. Sexual intercourse creates peristalsis. Next are the positive emotions. You have to think positively. If you hate yourself, if you're filled with fear, that's a good way to shut your bowel down totally. And the last one is to get into the herbs. Herbs are foods, too. Start using some herbs to get your bowel stimulated.

Dr. Schulze's
ORIGINAL CLINICAL FORMULAE
Since 1979

5 DAY DETOX
BOWEL
QUICK START DIRECTIONS

✔ **Promotes Regular, Healthy and Complete Bowel Movements which Prevents Disease**

✔ **A Powerful Intestinal Vacuum**

✔ **Removes Old, Poisonous and Toxi Fecal Waste that Causes Disease**

Congratulations! You have just opened the finest **5-Day BOWEL Detox K** available anywhere. More importantly, you are taking a big step to a new, muc healthier life. After cleansing out their bowel most people notice more energy an more vitality. They also notice improved digestion of food, better assimilation nutrients, and more complete elimination of waste. You will also be protectin yourself from disease.

WHAT'S INSIDE THIS KIT

- Intestinal Formula #1
- Intestinal Formula #2
- Air Detox

GUARANTEED RESULTS

"This program has proven itself effective in my clinic and in my customers' homes for over 25 years. I guarantee it is the most powerful and effective colon cleansing program available anywhere."

A POWERFUL, EFFECTIVE AND COMPLETE CLEANSING PROGRAM FOR THE COLON

The first step to powerful health and the best way to prevent disease is to clean out and detoxify your colon on a regular basis. Of further importance is to train your bowel to empty itself on a regular basis, 30-60 minutes after every main meal, two to three times a day. My **5-Day BOWEL Detox Program** will help you achieve both of these goals.

HOW TO BEGIN

The first thing you must determine BEFORE you begin this program is how often you have a bowel movement. That will decide how you start.

START HERE – If you are currently skipping days without having a bowel movement...

...start using the **Intestinal Formula #1** <u>only</u>. It is best not to rush and <u>not to use</u> the **Intestinal Formula #2** <u>right away</u>. Let's get your bowel working better first. The reason for this is simple. You are already a bit constipated and sluggish. Your bowel is not active enough to use the Intestinal Formula #2, which could constipate you even further. Don't worry, there are more than enough Intestinal Formula #1 capsules in your bottle to do this *and* complete the entire **5-Day BOWEL Detox Program**.

So start by taking one capsule of **Intestinal Formula #1** with or just after dinner. It is best to take this formula with food. If the next morning you do not have a good, complete bowel movement, or none at all, this evening take two capsules with or just after dinner. Continue to increase the dosage of Intestinal Formula #1 by one capsule each evening until the next morning, when you sit on the toilet, you have a complete bowel movement. A complete bowel movement may consist of a larger volume than you would normally see in the toilet bowl, or you may experience two or three intestinal waves of fecal matter elimination. So don't be too quick to get off the toilet. Your bowel movement may also be loose, even a bit like liquid at first. You may also experience a bit of gas or cramping. All of this is normal.

When you are having one or more bowel movements a day for an entire week, without skipping, you may now begin taking the **Intestinal Formula #2** (follow the directions on the next page). You must continue using the **Intestinal Formula #1** at your current dosage and even increase your dosage by one or two capsules when you begin the Intestinal Formula #2.

DIRECTIONS FOR DR. SCHULZE'S
5-DAY BOWEL DETOX PROGRAM

> "Never, never underestimate the HEALING POWER of Colon Cleansing."
> — Dr. Schulze

START HERE – If you have Intestinal Formula #2 capsules and are currently having one or more bowel movements a day...

...then you are ready to start using **Intestinal Formula #2** along with **Intestinal Formula #1**.

Simply take ten capsules, five times a day, for the next five days. You will be consuming 50 capsules per day for the next five days until the bottle is finished.

During this program, on average, you will be taking the Intestinal Formula #2 every two to three hours. Remember, when taking Intestinal Formula #2, you must drink a minimum of 16 ounces of liquid with or immediately after each dose. You may drink pure water, herbal tea or fresh fruit or vegetable juice.

IMPORTANT! While taking **Intestinal Formula #2**, continue taking one or more capsules of the **Intestinal Formula #1** every evening, with dinner or just after dinner. Most people under 150 lbs. need only one capsule, while those over 150 lbs. usually need two capsules. Intestinal Formula #1 does many things for your bowel, but most importantly it removes all the accumulated Intestinal Formula #2 from your bowel the next morning.

NOTE: If on the morning after taking your **Intestinal Formula #2** you do not have a bowel movement, increase your liquid intake today and also increase your dosage of **Intestinal Formula #1** this evening by one additional capsule.

START HERE – If you have Intestinal Formula #2 packets and are currently having one or more bowel movements a day...

...then you are ready to start using **Intestinal Formula #2** along with **Intestinal Formula #1**.

Simply take one packet, five times a day, for the next five days. Follow directions on the back of the packet for making your Intestinal Formula #2 drink.

During this program, on average, you will be taking the **Intestinal Formula #2** packets every two to three hours. Remember, when taking Intestinal Formula #2 packets, you must drink a minimum of 16-18 ounces of liquid with each dose. You may use pure water, herbal tea or fresh fruit or vegetable juice when making your Intestinal Formula #2 drink. Again, see directions on the back of the packet.

IMPORTANT! While taking **Intestinal Formula #2**, continue taking one or more capsules of the **Intestinal Formula #1** every evening, with dinner or just after dinner. Most people under 150 lbs. need only one capsule, while those over 150 lbs. usually need two capsules. Intestinal Formula #1 does many things for your bowel, but most importantly it removes all the accumulated Intestinal Formula #2 from your bowel the next morning.

NOTE: If on the morning after taking your **Intestinal Formula #2** you do not have a bowel movement, increase your liquid intake today and also increase your dosage of **Intestinal Formula #1** this evening by one additional capsule.

DR. SCHULZE'S
5-DAY BOWEL DETOX PROGRAM

IMPORTANT HELPFUL TIPS

Tip #1: If you are unfamiliar with what is normal bowel frequency, normal fecal consistency, you may think that something is wrong at first. You may also experience abdominal feelings that you have not experienced before. What you are used to is not normal or healthy.

If you have any concerns or questions about any aspect of this program please refer to my books **25 Ways to Have the Cleanest Bowel** (*included in this kit*) or **Healing Colon Disease Naturally**.

Tip #2: It took you years to become constipated, so take a few weeks or a month using my **Intestinal Formula #1** to get your bowel regulated before you begin doing my complete **5-Day BOWEL Detox Program** using **Intestinal Formula #2**.

There is no maximum dosage of **Intestinal Formula #1**. The record so far is 48 capsules in one day, so I am sure you haven't reached that dosage yet. Many people need six, eight or even twelve capsules a day to get their bowel working normally. But remember to increase by only one capsule daily. This way you won't accidentally discover the "laws of jet propulsion."

Dr. Schulze's NOTE: *"As a child I had only one bowel movement a week. That was normal for everyone in my family. Also normal for my family were severe bouts of constipation, hemorrhoids, kidney stones, heart attacks and cancer.*

*It took me 12 years of using my **Intestinal Formula #1** and consistent bowel cleansing to get my bowel working normally. Then for the last 20 years I have done my **5-Day BOWEL Detox Program** about every season, 3 or 4 times a year. I currently have 2 to 3 bowel movements a day, 20 to 30 minutes after every main meal, of perfect consistency.*

My point is that just because I inherited a dysfunctional, constipated bowel didn't mean I had to live with the suffering and illness that it caused me. With this exact program I was able to clean out and train my bowel to work perfectly. For me and my patients, great health was something we had to earn."

For more information about Dr. Schulze's **5-Day BOWEL Detox Program**,
see Dr Schulze's 2006 Product Catalog, or read
Dr. Schulze's book, Healing Colon Disease Naturally.

Call: 1-800-HERBDOC or Visit www.herbdoc.com

CONCLUSION

"Never, never underestimate the HEALING POWER of Colon Cleansing."
— Dr. Schulze

When I ran my clinic, new patients were often upset when I told them we had to start with a thorough colon cleansing. What they wanted was my secret energy pill, or youth pill, or something to make their insomnia, infertility, back spasms, headaches, diabetes, arthritis, whatever, miraculously go away.

Natural Healing is NOT about temporary quick fixes or pills to mask symptoms. It is NOT about cutting, poisoning and burning out disease. That's what medical doctors do. When you take that approach, often out of nowhere, your disease returns with a vengeance, much worse the second time around.

Natural Healing is NOT about Dr. Schulze healing people. It's about people HEALING THEMSELVES.

Natural Healing is about getting to the root cause of disease and illness, correcting it, and then building a healthy lifestyle so your body can do its best healing possible. Then you can enjoy a long, healthy and energetic life.

Dr. Richard Schulze

For more information on Dr. Schulze's 5-Day BOWEL Detox Program visit **www.herbdoc.com**, or read his book <u>Healing Colon Disease Naturally</u> available from Natural Healing Publications at **1-877-TEACH ME (832-2463)**.

A BIOGRAPHY OF DR. RICHARD SCHULZE

Dr. Schulze's Personal
HEALING MIRACLE

When Dr. Schulze was only eleven years old, his father suffered a massive heart attack and died. Three years later, when he was fourteen, his mother also died of a heart attack. Both were only fifty-five years old when they died.

At the age of sixteen, after a year of ill health, Dr. Schulze was diagnosed by medical doctors with a genetic heart deformity and deformed heart valves. The doctors told him that unless he underwent open heart surgery, his weak and deformed heart wouldn't be able to supply sufficient blood to an adult body and he would be dead by the age of twenty.

He declined to have the surgery and instead made it his mission to discover alternative ways to heal his heart. After three years of intensive self-immersion in Natural Healing programs and herbal formulae, he was given a clean bill of health by the same medical doctors who had told him he would die without surgery. His heart was healed. After curing himself of this so-called "incurable" disease, he set out on a mission to help others and enrolled himself into Naturopathic & Herbal College.

LEARNING From The Best

Dr. Schulze studied with the famous European Naturopath, Paavo Airola. He trained under, and then served an internship with, the famous natural healer Dr. Bernard Jensen. He also studied and apprenticed with "America's greatest herbalist," the late, great Dr. John Christopher, graduating to teach alongside him until his death. Besides having a doctorate in Herbology and a doctorate in Natural Medicine and three degrees in Iridology, he is certified in eight different styles of Body Therapy and holds three black belts in the Martial Arts.

GROWING From Experience

In the early 1970's he opened his first Natural Healing clinic in New York, and then later moved his clinic to Southern California. He operated his Natural Healing clinic in America for almost twenty years. During this same time he also managed and directed other Natural Healing clinics in Europe and Asia. In his two decades of practice, he treated thousands of patients, and in the second decade he became famous for his intensive

Natural Healing Programs and his powerful Herbal Formulae designed for degenerative diseases.

Spreading His HEALING MISSION

Dr. Schulze's Natural Healing Programs and Herbal Formulae are now used in clinics all over the world and have assisted countless numbers of people to create healing miracles and regain their health. He is considered an innovator, a purist, even an extremist by many of his colleagues, but to his patients he is considered a lifesaver.

Teaching and HEALING

Dr. Schulze dared to pioneer new techniques and therapies which went far beyond what most people thought possible with alternative medicine. The outcome of his work has been the achievement of miraculous and unprecedented results. His herbal formulae and Natural Healing programs are used in clinics worldwide to help people heal themselves of any number of supposedly incurable diseases. The positive results have reverberated throughout both the natural and medical communities.

Dr. Schulze has served as the Director of the College of Herbology and Natural Healing in the United Kingdom for eleven years and is also Co-Director of The Osho School for Naturopathic Medicine in England, France, and Spain. He has taught and lectured at numerous universities, including Cambridge and Oxford Universities in England, Trinity Medical College in Ireland, Omega Institute in New York, Cortijo Romero in Spain, and other natural therapy and herbal institutes worldwide. He has been the guest speaker at numerous churches and also on numerous radio and television shows. He is loved for his intensity, passion, dedication to students, sense of humor, creativity, and his exciting, enthusiastic, and evangelical style of teaching. He is mostly recognized for his unequaled understanding of Natural Healing.

Today... YOU BENEFIT

Dr. Schulze continues his healing mission today, revealing the truth about the unlimited healing power of our body, mind and spirit. After fifteen years of manufacturing his own herbal formulations in his clinic, Dr. Schulze opened the American Botanical Pharmacy in 1994, which manufactures and sells his industrial-strength, pharmaceutical grade extracts.

Dr. Schulze is also a leader in exposing fraud in medical, pharmaceutical and even herbal industries. To this day he continues to promote the message of Natural Healing through his videos, audios, books, and newsletters.

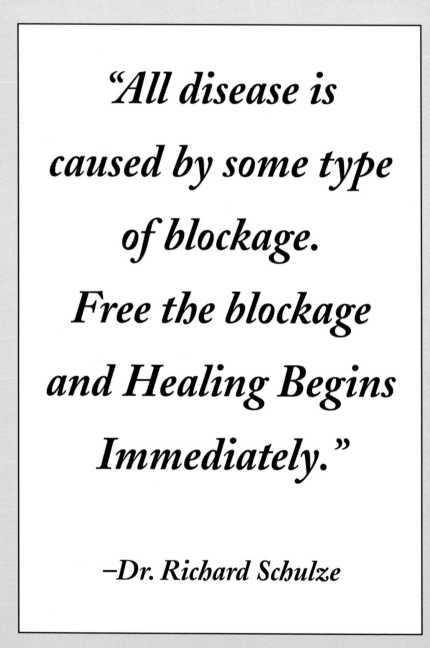

"All disease is caused by some type of blockage.
Free the blockage and Healing Begins Immediately."

–Dr. Richard Schulze